D0685072

TAP-ROOT

poems by

Indigo Moor

MAIN STREET RAG PUBLISHING COMPANY
CHARLOTTE, NORTH CAROLINA

Copyright © 2006 Indigo Moor

Cover art by Dallas Drotz, www.dallasdrotz.com

Acknowledgements:

The following poems have been previously published, are soon to be published, or have been acknowledged by contest:

Cave Canem Anthology VIII: "Harvest"
Cave Canem Anthology IX: "Disorder"
NCPS Anthology 2006: "Back Through the Storm Door,"
    "Ethos," "Apotheosis"
Eskimo Pie: "Splinter of the Path"
Focus on Writers Contest: "Mojo"
Gathering Ground: "Tap-Root"
Mochila Review: "Bound"
Poetry Now: "Of the Dirt"
Rattlesnake Press: "Uprooted"
The Comment (Boston University): "Metal"
The Ringing Ear: "Splinter of the Path"
Tule Review: "Splinter of the Path"
Xavier Review: "Nomads"

Library of Congress Control Number: 2006939549

ISBN: 978-1-59948-046-6
ISBN: 1-59948-046-8

Produced in the United States of America

Main Street Rag
PO Box 690100
Charlotte, NC 28227
www.MainStreetRag.com

Dedicated To:

Theresa Elaine
Sheila Renee
Judy Diana
Darryl Lothell
Erika Michelle
Josie Patterson
Rebecca Patterson
Rubynell Lomick

In Memory Of:

Kevin Jeranza
Miss Willie Bert
Minnie Mae
Woodrow Patterson
Richard Patterson
Walter Theron
Reginald Vaughn
Charles William

Special Thanks To:

My editor and friend *Star Vaughn*
All my *Cave Canem* fellows
The *SPC* Tuesday Night Workshop

&
Jack and Marty Hussey
for accepting me into your
house of wine and dreams.

Contents

IV. The Cast

V. Curtain Up

VI. Curtain Call

I. CALL TO STAGE

BACK THROUGH THE STORM DOOR

I left the South broken, a busted wing
and a crooked eye. Still, I wake mornings
with the taste of honeysuckle on my tongue.

The phone rings; voices weary with traveling;
wires weighed down with crows and thick heat.
I know it's the South, calling me to christen
the born or bury the dead —
Lord, I'm still addicted to its touch:

> *He doesn't have long. If you're*
> *going to come, it better be soon.*

In bed hours later, my mind still
taloned to the phone's bad news.

Weed, codeine, scotch. I've ingested enough
fog and brain-ash to black out the moon.
But the crucible of the past is relentless,
grinding behind eyelids. Memories spark
wild along the nerves' telegraph. The lens
focuses backwards and the mind grays decades.

I dream my past a fragmented play, spliced
together with rawhide ties and silk thread.
It grows claws and jumps the stage: a beast
my hands don't know how to tame.

There is no balm for the past's dull ache.
When the blue jay rolls up his song,
the whole damn world spins down on me,
falling back through the door,
I'm broken again.

II. DRESSING THE SET

Reconstructing Eden

you come upon the ruins of abandoned cities,
without the walls which do not last, without
the bones of the dead which the wind rolls away:
spiderwebs of intricate relationships seeking a form.
—Italo Calvino
"Trading Cities 4"
Invisible Cities

HARVEST

I worship these women of salt.
Backs curved, cloth-tied locks thick.
Hard beauty bent, jackknifing in fields
under a harvest moon fat-perigeed—
full crazy enough to kill them all.

Backs curved, cloth-tied locks thick
They speak harvest songs in tongues.
Stretch moan-hides across a drum voice
under a harvest moon fat-perigeed—
full crazy enough to kill them all.

Hard beauty bent, jackknifing in fields.
Scythe swing! Quails spring into trout-leaps.
Dark muscles swim through yellow waves
under a harvest moon fat-perigeed—
full crazy enough to kill them all.

BOUND

I remember most the dance of voices.
Song of leg chains kissing dirt.
Manacles arched rust rainbows
down to M'ssippi mud. Unsure
as young sailors, we tested our free legs.

Hungry-tense, dwarfed by black oaks
beneath a shifting sea of leaves
and branches, our feet cracked twigs.
A salamander jigged into underbrush.
Mother Lisa hummed a long forbidden
song, giddy beneath ferns.
This is freedom.

Never seen a map.
We knew railroads stitched states
together, hitched our train
northbound, while our numbers
whittled down to bonewood.

The M'ssippi grabbed Ezra's lungs,
weighted him down at a rough crossing.
We lost three to a mineshaft
dark enough to hang.

All of us camouflaged to fear,
shrunken into late, late gloom,
as a shotgun blasted Lisa
to a cypress. She hugged it
like touch was salvation.

I still dream her, a vine
straining to sky.
No longer able to climb.
No reason to. Dying,
at least, with her own name.
This, too, is freedom.

TILLING THE SOIL
Diary excerpts

☼☼☼☼

It is March and nothing has changed.
The tobacco swells; thick, leafy heads
thirst for sky, break the earth's skin.

The sweaty tangles of my hair tied back,
my sister and I cut leaves and stuff bags.
Momma swings the oversized hoe,

never quite striking where she intends.
Its rough handle callouses her touch.
The darkening circle of her empty

ring finger, a bad weather sign.
Sister and I found father's gloves
in the shed. She keeps them safe

for him beneath her apron. One day
we may give them to momma.
But not today.

☼☼☼☼

April brings the fat, grey caterpillars
of spring. They march the sky.
Pound their puddle-feet on the earth.

I sit by the window. Sister cuts
my hair into a wooden bowl—
memories grow weight, throb

11

the neck, and locks fall. The rain
is cold. Webbed together, withered,
the tobacco heads tremble.

        ✧✧✧✧

Beneath the sun's anger, May
is a wilted field; tobacco leaves
have dusted to wind.

The bare stalks are stunted
and resentful. The house wilts
beneath the bank's anger.

Ghosts squat in the bowl over the mantel.
Twist the hair around their limbs. Run their
fingers through our severed locks and chant:

> *My sisters,*
> *March turns May.*
> *We hold all our ghosts in*
> *the trembling of our hands.*
> *And really, what ever changes.*

SOLSTICE: THE PARTING

Summer, no less love
for fat Sol's tooth-grins and lies,
reaches for his hat.

UPROOTED

It took all our weight to drag the chain
over the stump, my brother

and I heaving links heavy enough
to strangle hope. Our hands lost

in grandfather's big work gloves,
slick grass betrayed our bare feet.

The tractor vibrated low. Hummed,
screeched, and began humming again.

Smoke marbled gray the blue morning.
Where we once played king-of-the-hill

on the stump's weathered face, we now
played Judas with an iron-linked kiss.

Grandfather spat *Red Fox*
tobacco, feathered the clutch once

to tighten the noose. The engine leaned,
a runner into wind, as the chain notched

deep into the wood, a lover's
embrace gone shockingly wrong.

The stump shuddered, groaned, wrenched
from the earth and tilted skyward.

I don't know what we expected.
There were no secrets.

No ghosts. No magic. Only
naked roots torn from the soil.

We stood with hands at our sides,
lost in the tremor song of earth,

all of us, broken like a promise.
Air so raw, it scratched our lungs.

Days passed, until once more we
circled the stump. Each of us secretly

hoped enough time had passed
for the love that married this stump

to earth to slip away. We then laid
axe to wood and released the rings.

IMMORTALS

The pond is a knot
sweetly tied. We imagine
tadpoles to whales,
believing we are gods.

A sweltering of heat
bends us into willows.
Black-heart horseflies
our mortal enemies,

but not one of us
brave enough to escape
through the mirror
of brown shimmering.

We tote a summer's
worth of sweat from one
bank to the other; we
mean to bring water.

Somehow we never
remember. As evening
bakes in, thick and slow,
we sit on the ridge

above the pond— black-
birds holding down a wire,
preaching day into night
with the clatter of our tongues.

CASTING ASIDE EDEN

Buried above my ancestors,
I kept their stories; they
dreamed my future,

necromanced life through
my veins, into my two hands
cupped around a crescent of soil.

That was before I traded
the horizon for the perfect shingles
of this new neighborhood: carved
from the wild; a bird shape
pulled from a block of wood.

Corn and wheat were sown to concrete.
Plowshares stagnated to flowerbeds.
Horses sold to memory.

I set my family's feet North.
Unhinged the moon, drug it
behind our caravan.

I hung it crooked in the sky
above my prefab roof, believing
I would hold its meaning as I
would all my ancestral stories.

Falling upon opiate grasses,
I was locust, sated—noticing
neither the moon nor my history
as they faded like the shrinking
calluses on my hands.

MOJO

It wails, gospel of the foothills.
Raspy voice, smoke, and thick chorus.

In the distance, the mining town awakens,
belches smoke in the Appalachian Mountains.

I burst out the kitchen into morning fog.
Screen door slams against the house.

Momma yells
You watch crossing those tracks, boy!

Empty, trailing me like a kite, my school bag
flapping. My thin breath wheezes through

clenched teeth into the swift curling haze.
New shoes struggle with the hill's dew.

Gangly legs and hand-me-down pants.
Baggy shirt, worn-shine collar, starched.

The whistle's banshee cry slips through
the mist's fingers as I claim the crest.

Mojo emerges from the fog.
Steel tracks dance, driven to frenzy.

Another long wail and the conjuring begins.
Mists pirouette and skip from the path.

Ghostly horses, bearing feathered riders low,
leap away from the lost vapors.

BOOM!
The engine thunders aside my thoughts:

No time for little boys and daydreams!
Clear the tracks! Clear the way! Mojo's

coming! No time for horses and feathers.
I got nothing but time to catch up to.

Loads of coal miners' sweat and fears.
Dark oils and widows' tears.

Time may forget these things,
But I got no time for such foolishness!

Who are you, boy? Were you here yesterday?
Who will it be tomorrow   if not you?

Strained from me—innocence seeps into
the rails—fueling the train, a mournful cry.

With one last wail, Mojo is gone.
In the distance, the school bell rings.

SPLINTER OF THE PATH

We drop hips and spin.
Dervishes locked in
a collective vision quest.

High-Top *All-Stars*
pound staccato
on dust-layered clay.

Sun-drenched, mad.
We forge rivers
of scarred flesh,
challenging the myths
of the playground.

Bodies twist skyward,
searching for a finger roll
sweet as Ice-Man Gervin's.
A jumper that can add
two more "O"s to smooth.

Orphaned beyond
ancestry, we yearn
for any rite of passage:
Drum of feet.
Dance of muscle.

By chance, we
found this Capoeira
of ball and hoop
and bled it black.
Now

Our dance is
Spin
for dark flesh mounds
beneath the small of the back.

Our chant is
Jump
for mahogany moons
swelled behind navels.

Our drum is
Stomp
for brown suckled nipples
between lips and fingers.

Our song is
Scream
for the places where we learn
the worship of all things round.

LATE SUMMER'S ELEGY

i.

Crisp summer thunder.
Heat lightning over the trees.
Not a cloud in sight.

ii.

Chill-morn pond mirror.
Darkness leans against the glass.
Lips exhale thick mist.

iii.

Street lamp serenade.
Moths dance to string light music.
Pale, cane-harvest dawn.

III. THE SCORE

Blue Notes in the Key of Mingus

Now
I have beaten a song back into you,
rise & walk away like a panther.
	–Yusef Komunyakaa
	"Ode to a Drum"
	Thieves of Paradise

NOMADS

For six days we purify metal,
sleepwalking through sulfur clouds.
A few pennies forged with every muscled
clang of pig iron and rust. Friday's
whistle, our Pavlovian call to bedlam,
triggers us down to dogs.

Come Saturday, we hang our checks
on new shoes, silk ties, gold chains.
Scrub iron ore from our fingers,
coke dust from faces before slow fading
from day to night. A bottle of gin
passes between us. We stiff-leg and
hip-drop a pimp down the boulevard;

tug our hats down until our faces
are curved horizons with brown, felt
suns rising askew. Walking the bricks,
we crave music worth killing for:
manna soaked in bourbon, grilled
over hot Mississippi coals.

The *Easy Lion Jazz Joint* exhales
an intoxicating vibration
of wood-stomp and tremor-slide.
Bass so cold it shatters hot breath.

The sax man's vibrato wrenches
moans from our bodies,
sways us into fevered cattails
wrapped in sweat and silk.
Spit-shined leather begins to fly.

Two more juke joints before sunrise.
A plate of ribs and a whiskey sour.
Sunday morning is a hangover
hard as an I-beam stove into our heads.
All too soon, the factory whistle.

SCHISM

Ma Rainey:
"Empress of the Blues" dead?
They lie. Never been no truck
that could cut Bessie Smith
from my side like a bad rib.

But it feels that way.
This morning my whole left side
hung broke like a cliff
half collapsed into sea.

Bessie&Me. Folks didn't know
we was the same person, split.
Schizoid: *A* and *B* sides
of the same vinyl 45 turned
slow. We both knew pain
would croon if it had voice.

Now I'm left, cleaved down
the middle, a wound
I can't stop touching; my days
filled with half-sung

    Blues

        that follow me through the house
        like pallbearers, heads bowed.
        Blues that lie drunk across the pale
        silence of phone. They sit in the corner,
        legs cradled, rocking to a deep-
        throated moan.

        Blues crystallizing the window's dew,
        bending the cold, gunmetal light of dusk.
        They settle quiet on the wall, a bad cloud

of insects; sprout on the lawn like scabs,
casting black seed into night.

Blues throb like blood blisters, climb
my body like wisteria, whispering
in a voice too familiar for me to ignore.

SAY IT AIN'T SO

Charles "Baron" Mingus:
Sift my ashes from the Ganges and I'm Harlem bound. There was a Renaissance. Night-shaded specters jittered and jived to me and Dolphy, my bass casing flung over my shoulder, gunslinger style.

The west-bound "L" slowdrags above abandoned shopping carts, broken whiskey bottles, empty tin cans; the steel wheel clatter of a Dannie Richmond solo.

A face silhouetted beneath *The Times* says: "Mingus is dead." But I pay him no mind. Moths dance the sodium lights of *Boogie Stop Shuffle* and *The I of Hurricane Sue.*

Three in the morning. Slicked-down jazz joints close like bloodshot eyes, squeeze out the last drops of watered down musicians. A heavy breasted woman traps *So Long Eric* in a down-flow of hair. "Go home, boy. Mingus is dead." I pay her no mind. *Haitian Fight Song* simmers over a big pot of greens and black-eyed peas.

My destination: 76th Street and Madison; a lost shrine. Cold stalactites of jazz-past hang from the ceiling, dripping chilled honeydew. A yellowed poster clings to the door:

> *Mingus tonight only! Get him while he's hot!*

Pale string of moonlight dangles through a broken window, quivers. Apparitions raise instruments, raise the blood moon, raise the night. Dolphy's horn speaks:

> *Mingus is dead.*
> *Play your bass, Charlie!*
> *Hold down the bottom.*
> *Drop it hard like coffee, black;*
> *Cigarette butts floating, cold.*
> *But find a new gig.*
> *Mingus is dead.*
> *Mingus is dead.*

TAP-ROOT

i

Concrete and steel drew the M'ssippi
back like a fist. Scythe blades swung
through dry harvests. Plows turned
soil hard enough to raise the Blues.

Muddy Waters sprang whole, dry-
heaved from the knotted center
of a plank-wood shack.
Shook hisself loose of blood,
dirt, moonshine, the ass-dark end
of a mule and was gone.

ii

Since, twisters have spun the shack
'round, bent its insides out, 'til it
vomited its secrets on boot-dust roads.
Now tourists use splintered slivers
of history as toothpicks.

A little ways down the road
you can squander a week's pay,
Sleep in an old slave shack.
Spend a day picking cotton.
Smile for pictures.

iii

The M'ssippi used to cover
these parts, until they dammed
it up, held its tongue like words
you choke back in church
to keep your insides from escaping.

Staring across dusty fields
you can ache the need for river.
Almost drown in longing for Waters
that won't come here no more.

TINDER

When the music rising
arcs the sunset into disbelief,
it's time to sweat away
what kills us in the day hours.

At wood's edge,
the candlelit shack and
its jackbeat pulse—
its black-rhythm heart—
its pale-veined wood.

Through the door glides
a dress, lily-struck bright
and flowing. We touch hands
and the petals open in a spin.

By midnight we have covered
and recovered each other's
steps with grace. The light by
which we dance: candle's breath
lapping at our heels.

Our other selves, the daylight people,
in this place are nothing more than
        dry kindling heaped
        on a funeral pyre—(burn sweetly)
        a crippling shame
        of darkened skin—(burn fiercely).

Armored with smiles,
hothouse tears lace our cheek
as we dance
the sacrifice of flesh.

At least,
this immolation is honorable,
saints and demons
have perished this way: frenzied,
                    spent, ablaze.

ANOTHER MAN'S BED

*Robert Johnson, seeking out older, often less attractive
women, or a homely young girl, for whom there would
likely be no competition, would exchange his attentions
for their kindness and a place to stay. Johnson was a
reputed ladies' man to whom women "were like motel or
hotel rooms."*

—Alan White, *Robert Johnson's Life*

My dream is always:
I wake to a ruptured silence,
an icepick cracking my dream slumber.

Impulse says
Get your shoes.

Keyhole has sucked daylight
from the room.

Get your shoes.

Left hand sweeps the floor
beside the bed.

Is this how death catches me?
One hand lost in dust?
Where are my shoes?

Dim streetlight glow pushes
through the window,
graying the room.

My eyes become focused rods
divining shape from shadow:

Someone has polished my wingtip
shoes, granted them flight, nested

them on the dresser. The chair
in the corner now wears a hat,

grinds on a cigar. Its single,
smoldering eye finds mine.

Smoke climbs the air
like ivy on an invisible trellis.

A gentle *click* and a tiny hole
floats above the chair's arm:

deep, hungry, trying to drag
the room into its mouth.

Six chambered screams curled
like fetuses in lead wombs.

A silk-sigh, rustling of sheets
as she shifts beside me.

I lie unbreathing, an eternity
away from motion, wondering
which way rolls me into the grave.

ETHOS

The way the head is hung
low, resigned—heavy,
between the sloped shoulders,
concentrating. He sits

behind the piano
the only way he knows:
as if the bench were a tractor—
the broken-down spinet
        an unfurrowed field—
and there is a hard day ahead.

A strange summit,
this makeshift stage,
        to seek the majesty
of art and solitude. Erected
on sawdust and hay
beneath a strident sun.

Fingers tremble, an inch above
resonance:

After last planting, last
drought, time
hitched a wagon,
            gutted the farm
and left only these hands,
the hunger.

Yet he knows the precise
way the plow creases the land,
is not the only way
        love eviscerates, rips
a man to the heart of things:

inside him, somewhere
one song that says

I regret nothing.
Forgive my hands this failure.

LAST CALL IMPROV

My apology melts into vodka
and swirling ice. Her fingers lost,
trace the links of her necklace.

On stage, Cecil Taylor cuts heads
with his quartet. Atonal waves plug
the silences in our last dinner together;

two cliff divers on a dizzying drop
from grace. A rapid descent key change
closes her eyes. Cecil's fingers dig

into a flat B, drag us into the rhythm.
My breath grazes her ear. *Remember
when Cecil played that set*

at Smoke's in the City?
She leans away into stage light glare.
That wasn't him.

Cecil's fingers duel with ivory.
Keys obey. Heart pulp and blood fruit
stain the Steinway's checkered grin.

Her hand slips away as adagio
moves to allegro. Bass player growls
his wide-legged stance.

On the table, my returned key
is a whale beached beyond
the sweat of her glass.

The rhythm leans us into calypso.
Cecil stomps fire wood to wood, kicks
out the back wall, blacks out the sun.

Twenty years ago, she wore black silk.
I kissed her in a field before a rise
of quail against burnt red clouds.

Cecil curled smooth as incense from
my radio as we teased the xylophone
of each other's spine. The drummer

hits a trip wire, drags me away from
shrapneled memories. We snap
our fingers to the deep sweetness

trapped in our skin. There are still no
words we share. A tear rolls down her cheek.
She wipes it away before I can.

THE BETTER TRUTH

The mind stores that part
of history that glimmers,
glosses together the fragments.

Present day crow-speak
never remembers Armstrong
grew Dizzy with disbelief:

Be-Bop and all, so much noise.
Just as Miles's watch couldn't
catch the later Trane's grooves:

dissonant whistles, wheels
that kachinked in all
the wrong places. It's fact.

Still, meticulously, our
thoughts leap *Giant Steps*
'til we're *Sittin' In the Sun:*

single chain-note
molecules, DNA strings
we never question.

The unmade verity.
The altered dream.
We piece together

the shimmering oasis,
the better music
of the seamless lie.

Each tale a hatchery
for the almost—
truth remembered:

RAIL SONG

Three men can drive a railroad spike
With nine blows of their hammers.
—D. Edgar Murray,
Laying Down Track

I count my blows in threes.
Hammer song in the trees.

Sparks fly from the sledge.
Tremble my legs to the edge.

Another rail from the rack!
Carries my soul up the track.

Build my song on the hills.
Stop when the hammer's still.

Build my song on the plains.
Drive my body to a cane.

I count my blows in threes.
Hammer song in the trees.

IV. THE CAST

Origin of Ghosts & Lingering Apparitions

Everyone deserves a poem—deserves the metaphor
taking shape, trying to find the pulse of their blood,
to make music of their everything.
                          —Kwame Dawes
                          "Carolina Barbecue"
                          Cave Canem Anthology IX

DOMINO

Seasonal Affective Disorder—*A mood disorder associated with depression episodes and related to seasonal variations of light. Characterized by depression during the winter months, with symptoms subsiding during the spring and summer months.*

Seasonal

2003 Cambridge, MA

I work seasonal contracts in New England,
before the snows, hoping New Orleans
calls me home. Autumn is the scent balanced
between asphalt and dying leaves.
I look for signs:

Nor'easter clouds strangle sunlight
to a whisper. The streets are lean,
pale mice stretching for burrows.
They tuck hibernating muses in their jowls.

Beggars exhale tendriled dreams,
stale to the touch.

My shadow has weighed me empty:
a smokehouse filled with ghosts
who dry inspiration on my tongue
like tobacco leaves at harvest. New
England is trying to call me its home.

Between two moments, the sky shimmers.
A silent horn quakes through the boughs;
flame-veined leaves begin plowing downward.

Affective
1985 Charlotte, NC

Beggars exhale tendriled dreams
stale to the touch, a winter's longing
stitched above their eyes. Buildings
halt sunlight and grant substance
to shadows. Hoarfrost manifests,
rides the coattails of every breath.

Someone remembers how summer seemed
locked in the clenched fist of a lump of coal.

Winter offers no apologies for air
that hangs dense, heavy as sin
dangling from southern oak.
The clouds are hushed as chameleons
as they slow-descend frigid pillars of sky.

On the streets, the pickings are scarce.
Pedestrians with necks bent to bone
rarely notice a mass of humanity shivering,
balanced on the line between here and not.

It's almost magical the way the homeless
coil around a corralled pocket of heat
no bigger than a hummingbird's egg.

A sock-gloved hand swipes a stray drift
from the top of a stolen shopping cart.
No amount of ashen-white snow
can camouflage a tin cup's barren womb.

Disorder
  1964 New Orleans, LA

Someone remembers how summer
seemed locked in the clenched fist
of a lump of coal. But that was January,

the coal man's swagger a quaked
rippling of white thunder. Winter
dwindled sharply, thinning his pockets.

But it would never thaw his contempt
for us. Cocksure as Prometheus,
he held fast the secret of fire.

Coal chutes were ebon whores
choked to whimpered protests,
jaws clanged shut afterwards.

With us children, he deviled
every chance encounter: *The cops*
gonna arrest your brothas

and sistas at the protest today.
Throw their black asses in a cell
way back in the jailhouse.

His father owned the delicatessen—
sandwiches thick as come-all rendered
tables swaybacked and bowlegged.

His contempt for us as palpable
as his son's. For weeks our voices
had been sirened inert by too many

sunless days. One morning, winter
broke and the morning dove's song
slipped smelling salt under our skin.

Police cocooned the store in nightsticked
layers. Protesters encircled the mass,
incubated it to a malignant cyst.

We children stood, fingers hooked
to white-knuckled clench, gleaning truth
through the links of the playground fence.

Silence

A brick somersaulted through a spike of sunlight.
A nightstick rounded into a hollow of flesh.
On the delicatessen's brick wall,

slick, scarlet flowers began blooming, each one
bright as the summer leeches we peeled
from our skin and burst between our fingers.

BETWEEN JOBS

The ass end of a Boxer was
an easy job. At sixteen, I did it
badly—playing at grown,

waiting for college on the night-shift
of the cardboard factory. Dead trees
were cut, perforated and folded

with half-ton kisses. Shaped into boxes
for watches, appliances, foods.
The foreman balanced the quota.

Flickering, florescent lights. Endless shifts.
Fibred dust storms devilled our lungs.
We fed and tended the Boxers:

metal mastodons chained to concrete.
Blood-oil spun in transparent gear covers.
At the ass end, I herded ten boxes

per batch, lassoed them with an almost
smooth, elliptical pull of twine.
A quick slice from my ring knife.

My fingers knew the work, but my mind
grew dizzy beneath an endless vertigo
of boxes, falling toward me like bad

trapeze artists. Every 30 or so batches,
someone would have to catch me up.
My grandfather got me this job.

I couldn't quit. Beneath the moth-tainted
glow, nights melded into each other. Even then,
I knew my body meant for muscle work.

I knew my mind destined for rigid reasoning:
I could stack a wall of heavy boxes tight
enough to erase seams   or untangle a knot

of equations into a line straight as a desert horizon.
But I was still young, unjaded, dreamful,
and absolutely no good at between work.

SHEPHERD

At the intersection, he sells the Persian lilacs
grown from someone's garden. He smiles, gives
change as exhaust turns his lungs to ash.

For 30 years, he was a school crossing
guard. Slick corduroy and cotton-friction
warred beneath neon chain-mail. For 30 years.

It is said: a shepherd forever tends his flock;
the herd instinct always strong. Every afternoon,
a clock brims in his eyes at precisely 3 p.m.

From the mercy of distance, he is a mannequin
awkwardly balanced. Head thrust forward. Chin,
a divining rod mapping the path back to the school.

At the playground, children are chaotic
blurs cartwheeling past his vision.
A young, female crossing guard patterns
the traffic to her slender-handed rhythm.

But his mind is tuned to a dissonant waltz;
Slow down he says, but his voice is swollen
shut, his mouth a pasty whispering of blue.
A pantomimed speech only the lilacs can hear.

THE BLACKSTONE MURDERS

"Your eaves, attic,
even the chimney;
everything's infested.
Happens in old houses.
Bird shit. It's like
strong acid to fresh
paint and primer.
We can't start painting
'til the birds are gone.
For a little extra, we'll
get rid of them for ya."

For three days
we tried to ignore
the scent of almond.
The pale, tortured rain
that shrieked and fluttered
in circles to the ground.

Wood, brick, sidewalks,
everything molted.
The trees sweated
sticky-brown, gaudy
and reddish. We
wore galoshes
to the mailbox.

I asked around,
learned other ways:
You can relocate
the nests. Get rid
of the eggs.
Block the holes.
Lots of things could
have been done.

One morning,
taking out the trash,
I found our cat—
stiff, wide-grinned,
feathers in his teeth.

Armed with a shovel,
broom, and grimace,

I collected beaks,
skeletons, cat fur,
chips of dried blood.

The day they came
to begin sanding,
I fired the painters.

A month later,
when the pigeons
returned, I put the
house up for sale.

RECKONING

I remember
        this mostly
as I remember
the way bits of onion float
      lazily at arm's length
beneath warm sink water

being separated by a thick-
handled knife,

the way memories are taken apart
after they grow slim, lose cohesion
and separate, then
        drift the years.

The Thompsons' little boy
was missing for four weeks
      before they found him
behind a dumpster.

And so six of us
became pallbearers,
at ten and eleven years.

The cemetery gates, ivory-
grappled,
      plastered to the walls.
Open, hungry in the manner only
such gates can be.

The graceless coffin, ungainly,
      the polished handles,
the long, wide marble steps.
One of us stumbled, just a
little, and we all giggled.

Swaying beneath the weight
of this child's coffin, the right proportion
          for pictures, from a distance
it would all seem so normal.

METAL
The Tow Truck Driver's Lament

Atilt, run aground on the highway's
graveled shoulder, you've buried
the prow of your car into the guard rail.

How long did you curse your luck,
offer prayers to metallic steam, black
exhaust, and a coughing engine block

before you called me?
No matter.
I always come.

I rechristen it male,
this vehicle that lies broken—
like all the men in my life:

My father whets his tongue
on grindstones. One uncle worships
stained glass saviors. Another

hammers scrap metal into panthers
and giraffes. Dreams of Africa.
Wants to die there.

They taught me to sing Doppler
music, the breakdown lane's
sporadic composition.

I step down from the cab.
Your name shrinks in your throat.
It's not my size that frightens; it's my hands,

heavy enough to drag sunlight
from the sky. When my boots punish
gravel, folks lose all their tongue.

I relish the dressing of your polished grill:
insect husks and dried pigeon guano.
Wind-thrashed heat swirls, shakes

the hood's greasy underbelly.
The reed-thin prop rod, slightly buckled,
above the gurgling radiator.

Belatedly, you offer your hand
and your name. I grunt and grind
30 years of dirt and angst into your palm.

I grew up amongst hard men, brandished
bottles of raw whiskey in cars that growled
deep, their bellies low to the ground.

Men of sun-scorched bronze
who loved the blood night.
Howled at pretty girls sashaying by.

You're speaking again, giving me
rhetoric, as if you are necessary.
This jagged canvas of twisted metal

begs the calloused brush. My hands
lend prosody to broken glass, draw
hip-street-jazz from beneath a broken chassis.

Somewhere there's a sonnet
in this heat-stroked carnage.
And you are no good to me.

Yet, it all balances.
My calluses play counterweight
to your skin's grace. My back,

annealed in the hot and cold running
gaze of fathers and uncles,
never bends. It's a science.

We're careful, men like me;
it's always the inner pressures
that break us. Once cracked, no

bandage will mend, no sutures will take.
We leak steam 'til we're hollow,
and we're damned hard to love.

SHELF LIFE

The emergency room doors swoosh open,
usher in a gurney and a murderous heat.

It swells the air conditioned corridors,
peach blossom and milkweed walls.

There's optimism on the EMT's face, but
I'm a preacher. Forty years in the pulpit.

One look and I know: no one can save this
boy from the bad luck marbled into his skin.

I rub swollen knuckles, open my bible. Crack
loose a specter of the faith once woven there.

Now, rheumatic sinew and stringy cartilage
puppet hands that no longer dance the stage.

The patients' families always want a miracle.
I hover for hours over passages dizzying

as a roulette wheel, a broken centrifuge that will
never separate twilight from their son's blood.

The doctor swings the ER door measuredly
open. Raises cold stones in their stomachs.

One last prayer, condolences, I drive home brittle,
searching the split-ochre horizon for answers.

TINDER #2

A man burns
unnoticed in Harvard Square.
Listing, ablaze on the corner.
A borrowed cigarette
unlit in his mouth.

> *Brotha, you got a light?*

His lips are scorched, cracked.
Iron skillet dark. Kindling
catches behind his eyes.

> *Nah, I don't smoke.*

He eyes me as a mark.
Sparks leap from his tongue.
Hair erupts like breasted robins
streaking the dark edge of sunset.

> *You got a dolla, brotha-man?*
> *I just need one mo' to finish my Ph.D.*

The dollar crumples into the basin
of his cupped hands. Smolders to bone-ash
amongst the fired stones of his fingers.

> *Thanks, man.*

He grins, wide-mouthed.
Tongue splits like a pomegranate.
Steam rises from the crevice, ghosts him
as he darts down the subway stairs.

V. CURTAIN UP

presenting

The Displaced Child

Come, brother, come. Lets lift it;
come now, hewit! roll away!
Shackles fall upon the Judgment Day
But lets not wait for it.

—Jean Toomer
"Cotton Song"
Cane

UNSPOKEN

N'Orleans cradled John's first cry, but offered no path for his feet to walk.

Coffee-kissed-pale in a family hued Cajun-smoke, John buried his loneliness in Coltrane and Parker, held his sax tight to his chest, waited for the train's whistle to call his name.

His older brother, Eli, was dark as lovers' shadows; the French Quarter sweetened him darker, then ate him whole: Eli-swift, Eli-smooth, he of the quick smile and quicker hands, completing circles John longed to enter. Eli-damned, kneeling in back alleys where trashcan fires illuminated hearts best left to shade, crouching in rings where tumbling dice closed the distance between blue-blood and blue-black. John's job was to fill the mouth of the alley. The alarm-man, the whistle-man, trumpeting the tap-tap-tap of N'Orleans' finest: Armstrong for when the cops came from east ways, Bird for when they sneaked in from west.

Just whistle like you supposed to, John. Only thing you good for, anyways. You know I'll split the money with you later. But don't ask 'til we get home. Not in front of nobody else.

Eli imagined he must love John. Must love some piece of his mother in that smile. But he tired of protecting the white in his brother's skin. Punching back the rumors of Old Man Nelson on top of his mother when she worked as a maid on the high side of town. Surely, he must love John. But only when he could forget the other man in his brother's face. The man that made his father stand in the courtyard outside their tenement, teeth clenched, staring at the sky.

John loved Eli. Wanted nothing more than to be his older brother, who couldn't step wrong or talk strange, no matter the company kept. But a string pulled tight between them. John couldn't understand the fists Eli curved his way after defending him. Or the apology later, easing down from the top bunk in the dark of their bedroom, his brother's words soft, tongue a butterfly gliding lazily in his mouth. Then, always, a confession. Something dark for John to keep. The absolution only a brother can give.

At his post at the mouth of the alley, gazing over his shoulder to hunched forms silhouetted by fire dance, figures swaying beneath the gaze of the concrete Madonna, John wondered if rings would always be closed to him.

Wondered if circles would be his undoing.

CAMEOS

Eli:
You mad? Roll my eyes
backward. Painted in my skull,
freefalling through clouds,
two halo jumpers, tangled.
Brother, it's hard to love you.

> *John:*
> Brother, you see past
> my absence of dark only
> when trouble calls. I
> want to be more than just the
> dice you throw when things go wrong.

FLIGHT

Pretty Brown the men called him by the time he was old enough for it to be decent. John's brass held tight his grip on the Creole jazz scene. *Pretty* was the name given his sax. *Brown* for the hue of his skin, barely a shade lighter than the paper bag stapled to the doors where he played.

The bag? Just a joke, man. Don't think nothing of it.

But the bouncers creased their eyes to it whenever a patron's skin was close to low class. Pretty Brown's breeding was a close call in the best of lighting. In low candles and lantern glow, his name would always get him through. He was charmed that way, moving in the right directions.

Coming home in the early hours, John hid his sax in his bag. He slipped past the brothers' taunts of him of trying to *pass*. Thin lips tight, he kept his cool, stuck to his plan, put all he earned beneath the loose floorboard beneath his bed.

Always he came in well before Eli, who snuck in with the sun when he came home at all. Smoke and liquor hung in tatters from his breath. Staggering through the door, not bothering to risk the climb to the upper bunk, Eli stretched out on the floor, mumbling to John about the latest heist, the latest con. John kept one ear to his brother, the other to the window; he listened to the northbound 67 wailing in the distance.

MOTIF

John:
It is time to close the door on N'Orleans.
Drag down that indolent sun. Lay to rest
these wounded retreats and displaced dreams.

I call upon my recollections to succumb
to a burial spell for remembrances spent.
They come, honeysuckle & tar on the tongue.

They lean on a dust-swirled streetlamp,
suspended by a single strand of darkness.
Their faces sharpened on the damp

whetstone of pebbled blacktop. The boulevard
that was our home emanates ghostly scent
of dirt, angst and innocence marred.

I call them brother. They dance to Ohio Players
and Sly & the Family Stone in slow marionette
poses, spotlighted by fireflies. Each labors

to mimic the rhythmic sway of whiskey in bottles.
Their shoes are polished souls: black, wet and spent
as an old kettle. The hand-wrought iron mottled

by morning dew. I douse the fire, my upbringing.
The embers spark once and my heart is a cord
stretched in regret. Carved in me is a longing
that melancholy saxes only lean toward.

ELI&JOHN

*"The gods changed both [Keyx and Alkyone] to birds
[kingfishers]; the same strange fate they shared, and still
their love endured,"*

—Ovid, Metamorphoses 11.742

Rain is vapor, becomes. Then
back to rain. The legion eyes
of two watery phoenixes; lost,
what they must see, know.

Where both once christened God's
brow, now they usher guttered
sludge. What offense, what sin
for a torment so exacting.

The shared judgment: cyclic
curse of the Lazarused soul—
eternal circle from cumulous
temples to blind-fish caverns.

Rise. Now fall. Now rise…
Again. Each ascent brings
revelation: for both, eons
are remembered. On descent,

their minds lessened, rendered
myopic. Lost is the memory
of ages. Replaced by a sliver
of air, a single patch of earth.

CARRIER

She was coal dark, street-
wise, mesmerizing—
an acid-core diamond in raw brilliance.
She was stone eyes and prescience,
always a step ahead of Eli's thinking.
Berry-thick lips and a jack-death smile.

She was cursed—
An ebon-shelled serpent whose withering
scales flaked inward, the flesh emulsifying.

She was given to cracked fits,
coughing through junkyard curses.
Her teeth, flawless.

She shared her curse
pulled from a diseased needle,
casually, in sweat-kisses and satin sheets.
She knew her death
as surely as she knew
her hold on Eli.
She kept both close to her side.

AFFLICTED

Eli:
Cursed my flesh, those eyes.
Damn, that voice. I never could
hear Blues approaching.

CHICAGO: BLUES-TOWN JAZZ

Another sun
                down. God
cocks her hand, slow skips the moon
UP
The viscous night sky.   A two-hop, dead
Stop,
               hangs from the ceiling,
pure drop of liquid strange—a knob
      God grabs and twists, tunes
to a Hi-Fidelity
      blush of burgundy. Muuuuuu-zick
radiates outward, slides over con-
      vulsed ripples of clouds.

A halo of stars flash-nod cold,
hot
fusion
attitude.
      A thousand, thousand twink-
                          ling fingers
snapping white, blue,
green across the scene. But that's

    up there. Down on earth. Tonight. Every night. It's all about Blues. Creaky blues, floorboards loose. Rent is due. Wingtip shoes in hand, John tiptoes past the landlord's lair, eyeing his Dali-esque reflection carved in that bloodsucker's doorknob.

    This ain't no new news. Shell games are the same no matter if they're played on French Quarter streets or front office desks of jazz clubs: money flows faster some ways than others and the greener circles still beyond John's understanding.

Ain't no blues like Rent-Due-Blues. For John. Tonight. Every night. It's all about Blues. The nights: barely surviving his dream. The days: always dreaming of home.

OPUS MANTRA

John:
Too many beds know
my name. Lord,
        won't you ease my pain.
Sure tired on this road.
Tired on this road.

FIRST, THE CITY DREAMS A MAN

Chicago starts to look like me
the longer I sleep. My dreams
are dung-colored gates—closed,

a picture show plays on the wood.
A wicked-cool film full of subtext.
The important parts always fall on cracks.

On the streets, everybody knows me.
Even the people that pass by
with bumper stickers on their foreheads

 that say "Esplanade, Elysian Fields,
and Almonaster." Places in N'Orleans
I could never spell correctly awake.

Back home, folks dream my name, hop
747s and land on 122nd & Membrane Ave.
They sit in cafes, buy strong coffees—no cream,

no sugars—and wait for me to arrive
so they can walk by looking straight ahead,
pretending they have someplace else to be.

And that's okay, because all my best cities
are inhabited by beautiful people with purpose,
pretending they don't know me.

We pass each other's yearnings, waiting
out the moment when the dream turns
and everything falls into place.

My head is a lucid city filled with dung-
colored gates. Passages home disguised
as beautiful people and achingly bright buildings.

None of the gates are for me. I watch people
climb through each other's beautiful eyes,
melt into a building's bright face exclaiming

*Ah! Now I understand   &   the house is just
like I remember!* They clench tickets in the
closed circle of index fingers and thumbs.

Recognize each other by these inverted, communal
OK's that signify they are more than ghost screams
& echo bruises—*life.* It leaves marks.

THERAPY

George "Slim" Thompson:

Resolute, a metal fist creasing the clouds, I came back to N'Orleans. Touched down, feet knowing the streets. I find the unmarked glass doors, sit in the bar, sip water and ginger ale as a hard sunset rusts the evening. Above the Jack Daniels bottles, the TV flickers, two behemoths shuffle-dance. Leather gloves fly, attached to glistening pistons. Apache dancers craving love through swollen eyes. "First Time I Met the Blues" crawls out the jukebox. Another hour passes before he appears. You can't slit a throat with a glare. Can't plant a cancer in another man's chest. My anger narrates:

> *The antagonist enters, tired, listing: a crop-duster strafing a bar stool. He banks left, misses the seat, rights himself. Plants his faded jeans on the torn leather. Digs both hands into the bar.*

Ten years ago in the alley behind this bar, he wore a mask. I didn't need the box cutter he waved to carve his voice into my mind. I grew up with Eli and his brother John, fought Eli on the playground enough times to drag his face from under the mask, pull his name from the alley into the revelation of streetlamps. He didn't need to cut me. He did, anyway. The severed tendons of my hand, snapping back into my wrist like rubber bands. These days, I struggle to lift my son.

Let it go.

No. Some hate only knows how to grow. Preach me years and I'll toss them in the boiling pot. Lecture me scars and I'll shine them like shoes. Hours later, he is small on his stool: a boxer slouched into himself in his corner. He pays his bill, struggles with the nubs of the ring finger and pinky lost to the streets.

Not my problem.

He pulls a few dollars from his wallet. A faded picture. His brother lost to Chicago.

Not my problem.

The jukebox dies quick and he is shown the street. I follow him out the into streetlight glare. My hands creep into poisoned bricks. He staggers around lit corner after lit corner, finds every late night straggler and indigent; luck guides him through a gauntlet of almost deaths. Under a broken streetlight, road swept clean, he reaches his car, leans against the door. My arm closes around his throat and I pull him back into an alley. *You're dead, Eli. Been dead for years, you just didn't know it.*

He goes limp, leans against me like a child. *I'm sorry* he cries. I slam him to the ground. My boot digs into a rib, pushes a groan from his lip. I kick him again. Once to the head. He doesn't move. *Fight back, damn you.* He flattens against the worn pavement, head in dirt and sludge, hands spread. I want to step on them. Break them. Make him scream. Again comes the apology: *I'm sorry. Whoever you are. I'm sorry. Kill me if you have to. I'm sorry.*

I sit in my car, unraveling. Tug slowly away from the curb. Night air pushes through the grinding of my teeth. I turn back for my hotel, hating myself for not coming back in time to break the man. Cursing myself for waiting too long.

PULL

I am told it was moonlight that ripened
your failing heart until it finally
cracked, sent the clockhands spinning

off your flesh. I was a coward, still 3,000
miles away, convincing myself that if I
came at all, I could never catch the dying hour:

arrive too late and reconciliation falls
on upturned soil; arrive too soon and
stuttered gushings peak, then sour in the air.

Forgive me, brother. For decades, your
name has stretched my tongue to breaking.
But love and pain often anguish logic

Long ago, on a night like this,
I watched uncle rocket a coyote
skyward with a fistful of buckshot.

It slammed to the ground twisted,
skidding across the grass. Somehow,
it didn't know it was dead.

Front legs pawed the air as if leveled
by nothing more than errant moonlight.
Chicken feathers lined its muzzle.

It mewled, eyes tunneling through me
to the underbrush where its mate stood,
crosshaired down uncle's barrel

and already dead by every book and clock.
The mate stood, mesmerized not knowing,
in this world, every fool carries a twin heart.

Bang! I shouted and the underbrush
went wild with the mate's running. Still,
if animals have souls, two died that night.

Uncle cursed me under a killing sky.
*Why, Boy? You know she'll hit
the coop later. Don'tcha know that?*

This is my understanding
of the fear and silence
of these wounded nights:

the moon snares in the sweet
spot of the throat. Everything
that lives on is trapped in love.

VI. CURTAIN CALL

APOTHEOSIS

There is an extra star in Orion's belt.
I arc my mason jar up through the fading
light and snatch the firefly in mid-pulse.

The heat lightning's a distant sweetness.
Sugar-pink throbs on nimbus clouds
draining from the night's basin. A screech

owl's cry hugs the pine-peaked horizon.
Behind me is an aluminum *whoosh!*
A swing, a miss, a curse.

In firefly baseball, the elusive
lime-green flickerings mock us all.
Blind in the graying, we are forever

doomed to swing where they were.
We swear and corkscrew to the ground.
The tall, uncut grass plays slivered kite

to the evening breeze. Silhouetted, Momma
laughs at every exaggerated lunge, twist, and fall.
Her fingers are Promethean tongs that trap

each cigarette's volcanic ember. But tonight,
there is more flame than heart and hand can hold.
A twelve-firefly lantern pressed to my cheek:

Does my face glow, Momma? Do I shine?
Tomorrow noon, the rusted beak
of the weathervane will swing north.

Momma, summer,
the fireflies.
All gone.

Indigo Moor is a 2003 recipient of Cave Canem's Writing fellowship in poetry, Vice President of the Sacramento Poetry Center and editor of *Tule Review*. He is the winner of the 2005 *Vesle Fenstermaker Poetry Prize for Emerging Writers*. A 2005 T.S. Eliot prize finalist, Indigo has received scholarships to the Summer Literary Series in St. Petersburg Russia, the Idyllwild *Summer Poetry Program*, the Indiana University *Writer's Conference*, and the Napa *Valley Writer's Conference*. His work has appeared in the *Xavier Review*, *LA Review*, *Mochila Review*, Boston University's *The Comment*, the Pushcart Prize nominated *Out of the Blue Artists Unite*, *Poetry Now*, *The Ringing Ear*, the *NCPS 2006 Anthology*, and *Gathering Ground*. Indigo Moor is also a reviewer for *Black Issues Book Review*.